I t s b a m bi i playhouse

Disclaimer: names have been changed to protect the individual's privacy and identities.

I t s b a m b l i playhouse presents

Patience until your hair turn grey

Contents

Chapter 1 : relief 2 grief

Chapter 2: Stuck in a rut

Chapter 3: A walk of Remorse

Chapter 4: holding sincerity

Chapter 5 : giving additional efforts

Chapter 6 : inner thoughts..

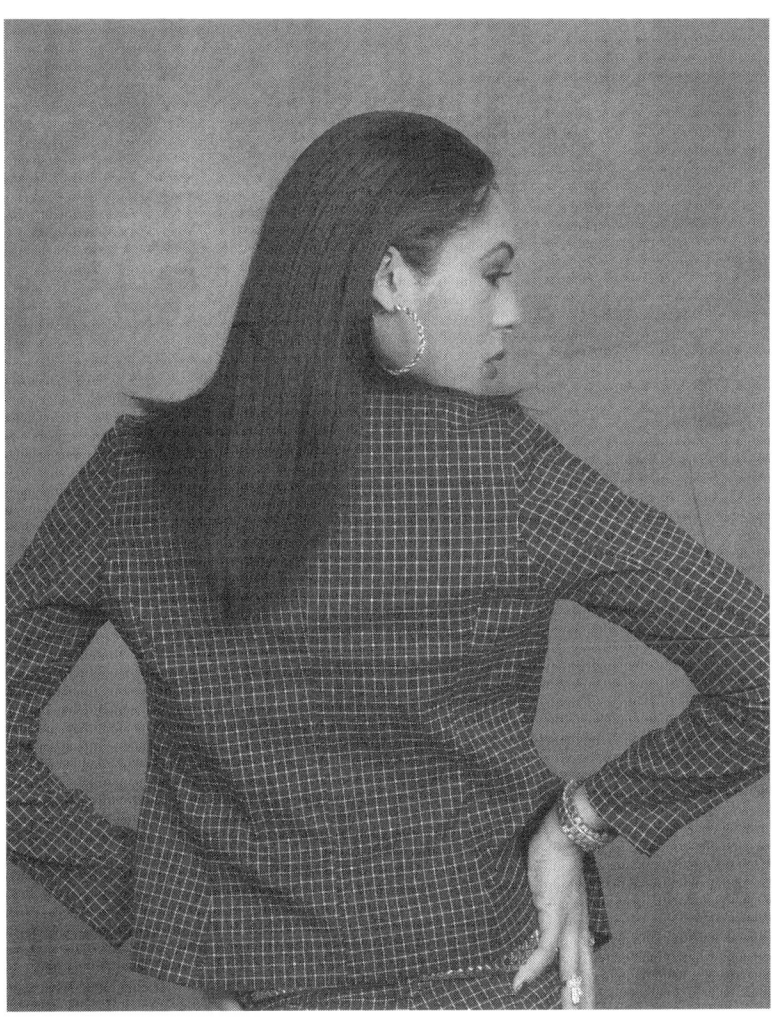

Chapter 1 : relief 2 grief

Locking myself inside my hotel room, I turned the TV off and sat in a pitch-black room. My mind was everywhere and I couldn't stop thinking about going back home to my mother's basement. At night when I'm trying to sleep there I can hear everything upstairs, and don't get me started on the furnace coming on in the middle of the night scaring me half to death and I pop up, turning my head as if someone was down there trying to get me. I'm grateful my mom let me stay in her basement, and that I wasn't on the streets, but I needed my own space. I was still in my hotel room, and just thinking about that put me in a bad mood. I cried and screamed into my pillow, then snapped myself back with the realization that I wasn't there at that moment and to enjoy my stay at this hotel while I could. I walked to the window in my hotel room and opened it as wide as it could go. My room was on the second floor and as I went to inhale the fresh air with my eyes closed, I heard a lighter flick and cigarette smoke came straight into my nostrils, which made me cough and I closed my window and went back to my bed. I lay there thinking, Something has to change and fast. It's easy to give up on yourself, but holding on and being your own motivation is the hard part. I tossed and turned, putting pillows over my head, trying to sleep but the noise wouldn't stop.

Literally constantly someone's car outside the hotel wouldn't stop going off, which made it extremely annoying. So finally after an hour of trying to ignore that I hopped up angry going to my hotel window, opening it up, getting ready to say, "Somebody, please come get yo damn car," but as soon as I was about to shout that out, the car alarm stopped and this older gentleman wearing a green sports jacket was walking to the hotel side door while holding his keys, which gave me the impression that was his car. I laughed to myself placing my right head over my forehead then got down on my knees and took a deep breath and counted to twenty-two. First I breathed through my mouth sucking up as much oxygen as I could to my stomach for five seconds, then held it in for five seconds, then let go, releasing that deep breath. Then I took another deep breath but this time through my right nostril while putting my left hand over my left nostril for seven seconds, then releasing it from my left nostril while covering my right nostril. I did that until I got to the number twenty-two then stopped. Having patience with myself I did that until my eyebrows stopped frowning. Then I told myself, God loves me, this isn't the end of my racing battle, but this is the very starting line, it's never too late to start again and get up. Nothing that I'm trying to get without putting any effort in is worth having.

I stayed in silence repeating that with my eyes closed and still on my knees. The hotel was right by the freeway and I could hear cars driving past and the trees blowing while the leaves and wind whistled in my ears. I could feel my face getting wet from tears falling from my eyes. I took another deep breath and counted to twenty-two and told myself, I promise to be more patient with you, and took a deep breath starting from my stomach for five seconds, then releasing. Then took another breath through my left nostril for seven seconds, then released it from my left nostril while covering my right nostril until I got to the number twenty-two. I finally opened my eyes and said "Patience, count to twenty-two." I told myself that the next time I felt my anxiety was messing up and when I felt I needed a little faith, love, gentleness, peace, self-control and patience, to just take a breath and count to twenty-two.

The next day I woke up and my heart raced so fast and I felt anxious. It was 9:30 a.m. and checkout was at 10 a.m., so I got up to take a quick shower to calm my nerves. Before I got in the shower I placed down a garbage bag in the tub so my feet wouldn't touch the inside of the tub. I could tell housekeeping didn't keep up with these rooms because the tub was dirty and it had a ring around it. After ten minutes in the shower, I turned the water off, getting out of the shower and grabbed my towel. Then walked to the bed to put on the clothes I had from the previous day. A grey jogging suit with my favorite beat-up boots. After getting dressed I gathered all my belongings then double-checked the room to see if I forgot anything. I didn't forget anything so I left the room and headed down the stairs to check out. When I got to the lobby I handed the clerk my room card then walked to my car and sat there thinking how I did not want to go back to that basement.

I looked at the freeway and just wanted to drive anywhere but there. I started my car then headed back home. When I got there I dropped my car off in the driveway and decided to go for a walk to get some fresh air. While walking for a couple of blocks, I sang out loud and told myself it was time for me to be in my own area again. I kept walking around further and further and saw this German shepherd off his leash while the owner was in front of the house doing yard work. The dog saw me and started barking coming toward me. My heart sank into my butt, and I started to run. I screamed as I turned around to look where the dog was and it was coming close with full charge speed with his tongue out. I turned down the block and hopped someone's fence and ran into the backyard then jumped another fence ripping my jacket, hiding behind their garage trying to catch my breath. I got away from the dog.

Trying to catch my breath looking at my coat ripped, I screamed in the air, "I can't catch a break." A guy in the backyard next to me yelled out, "Are you OK?" I said back, "NO! A dog was about to have me for lunch." He was an older guy and had to be in his late sixties from the grey hair and balding plus the wrinkles. He was barbecuing, and while flipping his steak he said, "I can give you a ride to where you need to go." I thought to myself for a second how I don't know this man and shouldn't get into the car with him, then thought about that dog chasing me and said, "Yes, please." He said he would bring his truck around to the front of the house I was at and to give him a few minutes so he could put his food away. I opened the gate to get to the front of the house and waited for him while sitting on the curb looking around to see if that dog might come back for me, but it didn't. I sat and thought, I should just walk back home, but another way, but I was so afraid of that damn dog. The man pulled up and was sitting out front in this red pickup truck and waved his hand for me to come. I opened the truck door and sat down in the passenger seat. When I sat down I buckled up then turned to him and said, "I'm Selena, thank you so much for this, you would have thought I had jerky in my pocket from the way that dog was chasing after me." He just looked at me while he drove and then locked the truck doors.

I looked out the back of the truck windows and as he got to the end of the block I saw the house with the dog. "That's the dog that was chasing me, that's him right there." I pointed while looking at the guy. He looked directly at the house and said, "I don't see any dog." The dog was clearly right there, you could see plain as day. "You don't see that dog right there?" I said while pointing toward the dog. "No, I don't," he replied, as he put on his blinker and continued to drive. "Stop the truck," I told him. He didn't stop. I unbuckled my seat belt and went to unlock the door. He looked at me and turned red as a stoplight and said, "What are you doing?" as he stopped the truck. I hopped out of the truck and didn't say a word. He kept beeping his horn telling me to get back in his truck and I told him "No, thank you, you've done enough." He kept saying, "Get back into the truck." I walked away fast, then he tried to drive the truck on the sidewalk where I was and I ran. I kept running until I got by this gas station and even then I ran inside.

I speed walked all the way to the back of the gas station and grabbed a water. I looked out the windows to see if I saw his red truck but I didn't see it. I let out a huge sigh of relief and went to the counter to pay for my water. I placed the bottle on the counter. "One dollar and eighteen cents," the guy working behind the cash register said with this strong accent. As I reached down getting the $1.18, I didn't have the 18¢ and the cashier guy said, "It's OK, no problem," while smiling and winking his eye. I could tell he was Indian and he had a ring on his big finger and had to be in his late forties. His belly hung over his shirt and his teeth were yellow like a rotten banana. "Thank you so much," I said while looking up at him and then walked to the door. He came from behind the counter as I was walking out and grabbed my hand while I was about to open the door and said, "Come back here with me." I told him, "No, thank you," irritated and went to open the door again, but quickly he grabbed my arm and said, "Please stay with me," as he walked closer to me. It was around four in the afternoon now because I looked at the clock they had in the back of the gas station. That quickly, while looking at the clock, he grabbed me by the waist and pulled me close to him while trying to kiss me on the lips, but I turned my hair, moving back and he kissed my neck. His lips against my neck felt like a cold, wet, slimy baby leach just landed on my neck. I went running out of there. I ran with my *water bottle in my hand and purse flapping off my side, so I just grabbed my purse to stop making that flapping noise. I finally stopped and opened up my water bottle than drank the whole lot. After I got done demolishing my water I looked up and saw that red pickup truck moving off the side of the street.*

Chapter 2 : Stuck in a rut

My mind was thinking run and run fast. I looked closely and it was him. The guy who had been trying to give me a ride. I paused and thought where could I run? There wasn't much time to think because he sped right by the sidewalk and said, "Hey, you sure you don't need a ride? I've been waiting for you." My mind went completely blank. I couldn't believe all this was happening to me in one day. From the tone of his voice, it seemed like he was genuinely concerned about me getting home. But I still wasn't about to mess around with him, so I told him my house was two houses down and that I'm OK and gave him a fake smile. He still was driving next to me as I was walking. I saw on the porch three houses down there was a man sitting there with his cat and I thought to myself, Act like you know him and walk up to his porch. I kept walking until I got by his house and said, "Hey, what are you up to?" hoping he would go along as I winked and slightly moved my hand back trying to let him know like I know you don't know me but please act like you do. He smiled with a confused kind of expression and then said, "I'm fine, and you?" I walked closer to his porch, placing my purse down on his step and sat down. I didn't look back to see if that guy in the red truck was there and the guy on the porch just walked on to look at the guy in the red truck and from his eyes moving I could tell he must have driven off as his eyes followed. "He's gone," the guy said.

I took a deep breath from my stomach, breathing through my mouth then held my right and left nostrils taking turns while counting to twenty-two in my head. The guy on the porch just looked me in my eyes and told me, "Don't be so afraid, you're safe with me." I appreciated that because he didn't even know me and helped me. I thanked him, holding in the sad, angry, annoyed and confused tears. I didn't understand why this was happening. I turned around and looked both ways behind me checking to see if he was really gone and he was. The guy asked me what happened and I explained: As I was walking and a dog started chasing me, I ran into someone's backyard and the guy in the red pickup truck offered me a ride. He seemed skeptical when I told him to look at the dog when we saw it while getting to the end of the block. So I hopped out of the car. He went on the sidewalk with his truck. I ran to a gas station nearby and was sexually harassed by this Indian guy. I ran from there and ran straight back into the guy in the red pickup truck, and how he helped me. He told me I should get some pepper spray and invest in a taser. I told him I already had a taser but I just didn't think I would need it. He replied, "You are going to need to keep something with you next time you walk alone, and if you don't have anything to protect you, walk with a stick or a fallen branch from a tree, pick it up and throw it at the dogs, all of them." I laughed and a tear fell from both of my eyes. I quickly wiped it up because I could see the guy feeling bad for me and I didn't need sympathy; I needed for my mind to be strengthened.

After I got done talking to the guy who helped me, I asked him what his name was and he told me "John." I thanked him once again and walked back home. I know that in learning, sometimes pain is the professor but I just felt so dumb while walking back home, I noticed my inner dialogue was telling me to feel this way. I already was having a weird day, so I decided to ignore those thoughts of feeling dumb and self-doubt and give my attention to good thoughts. I couldn't control what just happened to me so I decided to focus on what I could change. I reminded myself that at least I got away from all of those situations. When I got home I grabbed my stuff from my car then went to my room in the basement. I had rugs all over the floor from my apartment and candles so it wouldn't smell like a basement. I lay on my bed, which was on the floor and closed my eyes, thinking, Is this it for me? Then the furnace came on and I didn't even open my eyes. I was used to it now. I lay there with my candles on and listened to the rain sounds from outside. I wasn't changing my situation with staying in this basement, so was I choosing this? Yes, I was and couldn't be mad if someone wanted to come in the kitchen while I'm trying to sleep and the sounds of the floor vibrated to the basement. I wasn't doing anything to help myself get out of this situation.

I had enough pity for myself that just because this is my environment doesn't mean I have to adapt to it. I started to change my inner dialogue and tell myself, Hey at least you have a roof over your head, at least you are in a loved one's basement, not a stranger's. At least now you get to see your nephew grow. This is a temporary start, building step by step, you can change how you can get yourself out of this. Thoughts are powerful and become the way we view things. It was OK for me to have these emotions of feeling sad, depressed and angry about my situation but to not let these emotions take over, and let me see the good things out of it. I became optimistic and started applying at apartments, two-family flat homes and houses. The next day I applied for some more while waiting for them to call me back.

I became impatient and uncomfortable so I went back to what was familiar, smoking. Smoking calmed me and gave me a false reality that I was happy when I wasn't and made me not care. When I started smoking weed again I believed I needed it to deal with myself throughout the day. Instead of trying to understand my emotions of feeling impatient with waiting on a place to call me and being uncomfortable in the basement I just balled up my emotions. I would go to the garage and just smoke like every forty-five minutes. Even when I would be already high, I needed to be higher. When I didn't have it I became grumpy and a sour puss. I was still applying at houses but just kept getting denied. That just made me want to smoke more. If I didn't smoke I would lose my appetite. I felt I couldn't be creative without it and that I couldn't sleep without it. I was numbing myself. A couple of weeks went by and I still wasn't getting any callbacks for the places I applied to. I would make follow-up calls but every time I would talk to a realtor or apartment manager, they would either not have anything available anymore and I would be on the waiting list or I wouldn't meet the qualifications. This made me frustrated. I wanted to get high and go back to my false reality but I didn't have any more to smoke. All I had was cigarettes and they always made me get a headache so I didn't want to smoke them.

I decided to go for a walk to the store nearby but this time with my pepper spray in my purse. As I got inside the store I said hello to the lady at the counter and she responded, "Hello ma'am," with a big smile. I nodded my head and got what I wanted, a purple pop with trail mix. After I got what I wanted, I got in line. There were two lines, one with the lady I said hello to and another line with this other lady who must have just clocked in because when I walked in I didn't see her. I got into the line with the lady who said hello to me. In front of me was this man with a six-pack of beer and he kept turning around looking at me. I just looked down at my shoes because my mind was on getting me out of that basement. He kept trying to get my attention by making small talk. He turned around and said, "Yeah these workers here don't work fast enough, huh." I ignored him because I didn't notice them working and I genuinely didn't care. In the other line next to me was an older lady with her friend and two kids. I wanted to go to that line but someone just walked up behind them as I went to walk over there but then stopped. The guy with the six-pack of beer literally turned around and saw me as I went to move and said, "I'm going to let the girl with the big hair go in front of me." He said this loudly so that the whole store could see he was doing a good thing I guessed.

    I had my hair out in an Afro because I just washed it and combed through it the day before. I didn't say anything but I nodded my head and moved in front of him while he moved behind me. I put my things on the counter and the lady who said hello to me as I walked in started to ring off my pop but before she went to ring me up she stopped and looked up at me and said, "You know I know him, Sean he is a good guy, he didn't mean any harm by that." I just looked at her confused because I didn't get offended when he said that, I know my hair was out and it's not like he said, "I'm going to let him, with the big hair go in front of me," he didn't disrespect my pronouns. I didn't say anything to her. I just looked down at my purse and she continued to ring me up. Then the lady with her friend and two kids said to her friend, "I wouldn't have got offended if he said that to me." I just looked at her and she said, "What?" while putting both her hands out. I still didn't say a word out of my mouth. The cashier finished ringing me up and I paid and went to walk out.

As I walked out, the cashier said out loud, "Fix your attitude! What you don't know how to speak?" I still didn't say anything. I just walked out of the store. As I walked out of the store I just thought to myself how I wished I would've stood up for myself. Then I remembered that not everything needs a reaction, I was thankful he let me go in front of him and I should have just said "No, thank you" and let him go checkout but it didn't go that way.

Chapter 3 : A walk of Remorse

As I was heading back home I opened my bag and grabbed my purple pop. As I looked down to pull it out I noticed a tall guy walking on the other side of the sidewalk I was on. He had moved out of my way from a distance already and when we got closer to each other I looked down and when I looked up to open my pop he asked me, "Hey where are you going and where have you been?" I wasn't about to entertain him because I already was annoyed about what just happened. "Oh, so it's like that, huh?" He had on a button-up shirt, some khaki pants and some old-looking dress shoes. He looked older, around fifty-five from his patchy beard. "Yes, it's like that," I said while I kept walking. I shouldn't have said anything and kept my big mouth shut because he took it as an invitation that I was flirting, when I wasn't. He stopped walking and turned around, and I know he stopped walking and turned around because I heard his shoes make a scraping noise against concrete and he started walking behind me.

I turned around and asked, "Are you following me?" He looked me up and down smiling and said, "Yes … I am laughing." I told him angrily, "Please don't." I reached my hand into my purse and put my hand on my pepper spray getting ready to spray him if he came any closer. "Do you smoke?" he said. I didn't have any more weed so I thought to myself, OK, maybe I could smoke with him then leave when I get high. I looked at him and told him, "Yes," like an idiot. "OK, would you like to come over to my house and we smoke?" I didn't think before turning around and starting to walk toward him. "Let's go, where do you stay?" As we started walking toward his house he kept chattering about how he stayed with his sister and how he had six kids and his middle son was staying there too with him and that his sister had three kids but only one stayed with them. I didn't think too much about what he was telling me because I just wanted to smoke. He kept grabbing my shoulder saying, "What's a pretty youngster like you doing out here?" I didn't say anything back but he was giving me a bad vibe. I think he could tell because he stopped touching my shoulder and started introducing himself. "My name is Ronald, what's yours?" he said. I didn't look at him, I just looked toward the ending of the street we were walking and said,

"Lena." I didn't give him my whole name because I didn't want to.

He walked with a bounce, and as we got to the corner of the street, we went by a park and he said that his house was right at the end of the next corner just a few more steps. He started talking about football and how that was pretty much all he watched. When we got to his porch step he pulled out his key from his left pocket and put it inside the door. It was a small, brown brick house and it looked decent.

As he opened the door of his house it smelled like I was at the fish section of a grocery store. The living room had nice furniture and a big TV but that smell made me gag. From my facial expressions he could tell something was wrong and asked, "Are you OK? I don't want you to be uncomfortable, do you want something to eat or some water?" I told him, "No, I'm fine, I have my purple pop and trail mix I haven't even opened yet." I jiggled my bag letting him know they were there and he just nodded his head slowly and said, "Right," and let out a small laugh. "Let's go into my sister's room." I asked him why not his room and he didn't say anything. As we got into the hallway, his room was right before his sister's room. He opened the door to his room. "This is why," he said and opened the door wide. His room had clothes on top of clothes on top of other clothes, plates with leftover food, chip bags, restaurant bags, and a fish tank that had zero fish in it, that was where I was smelling the fish from.

"Ohhh, alright," I said, then he laughed and he opened the door to his sister's room. "My sister is out of town right now and I'm here with my middle son and nephew." He pointed to pictures on his sister's wall of her and her kids, and as I went to get a closer look I noticed that her son looked strangely familiar.

When I got close up to the picture I tapped it and two roaches came from behind the frame. I jumped back then shook it off. "The boy in that picture … what's his name?" He looked at me while turning the TV remote to football and said, "Frank, that's my nephew." I knew Frank from high school, he was friends with this boy I liked, Aaron. I grabbed my bag with my pop and trail mix that was on his sister's bed and shook it then walked out of the room to the front door. He followed me and asked, "Why are you leaving? We didn't even smoke yet." I told him, "I have to go," while trying to unlock the door. He grabbed my hand that was trying to unlock the door and said, "You can't leave me like that," with this expression on his face that he really wanted me to stay. "Ronald, move out of the way, I told you I have to go." I raised my voice, but he shushed me and told me, "Be quiet, my nephew is downstairs playing a game and I don't want him to tell his mom." That made me really want to go because first your grown and can't have company? And Frank knew me from high school and I didn't tell Ronald I'm trans and I don't know his views on trans women." Open the door now," I said.

He stood there for a couple of seconds then let out a huge sigh and turned around and opened the door.

As he moved away from the door I walked out. He closed the door and as I got to the house next door he was behind me putting on his dress shoes and zipping up his jacket. "Lena, come back," he said as I kept walking. "I seriously have to go," I told him while still walking but a little faster. He ran closer to me and said, "Here," putting this blunt in my face. I went to grab it because I thought he was giving it to me but he pulled the blunt back and said, "Let's go to the park." I thought we were just going to smoke at the park, so I started walking with him to the park that was nearby and as we were walking, I didn't say a peep; I just wanted to smoke really quick then go home. I should have just run away from him and gone home. I don't know why I was being so foolish. When we got to the park, he was walking in front of me and sat down at a bench. I sat down next to him. I closed my eyes, shaking my head thinking just go home. But I kept ignoring my thoughts. I heard his lighter flicking on and I opened my eyes and turned to look at him. He was flicking his lighter off with his left hand while holding the blunt and with the right playing with himself. "Suck this and you can blow this." He didn't seem like the same nice guy he was pretending to be anymore. He was serious. I went to get up and he stopped playing with himself with his right hand and grabbed my arm tightly and told me to sit down. I didn't want him to hurt me so I put my head down and did it. After I got done he stood up, pulled his pants up and started to walk away. He spat and kept walking while lighting up his blunt.

Chapter 4: holding sincerity

On my way back home I felt degraded and like a complete fool. It was around 11:00 p.m., the leaves on the ground blew in the wind as they crackled on the ground. I felt myself cracking, it was like my heart broke down the middle and my head became light. When I got home I brushed my teeth like twenty times and took a long shower closing my eyes trying to scrub off the mistake I just made. I knew better but I didn't do better. After I got out of the shower I walked downstairs from the bathroom to the basement with my towel on covering my breasts and body with no socks on, I forgot to bring a change of clothes upstairs. When I walked down the basement stairs I put oil on my body then put my pajamas and socks on. Then lit up one of my candles and lay my back down on my bed. I couldn't help but feel so uncomfortable with myself. I tried to fall asleep but as soon as I closed my eyes someone upstairs came down the stairs and woke me up. I could hear every step someone made upstairs and it made me even more uncomfortable.

    I decided to leave so I got up and packed my bag. I grabbed my blanket from my bed, and pillows, a change of clothes and underwear then went upstairs to get my toothbrush. After getting my toothbrush I went back downstairs to the basement to put my toothbrush in my bag and put on my burgundy jogging outfit. I headed to my car that was in the garage and put my bag in the car then went to open the garage door. I got back into my car and started it up then backed out slowly. When I got my car into the driveway out of the garage I parked my car and opened the car door to close the garage door. As I was walking to the garage I had my phone in my hands and as I went to pull the garage lever I dropped my phone right on the concrete. When I went to pick up my phone after closing the garage half of my screen was green from the screen being damaged and it was cracked all over. I didn't even care. I just picked up my phone and walked to my car and put my phone in the passenger seat. I backed out of the driveway and went to a motel that wasn't too far. I parked right by the entrance then got out of the car to walk toward the door the motel. When I got to the counter of the motel I said, "One bed for two nights, please," while pulling out my ID. The guy working the counter told me, "I'm sorry we are full for tonight but next door they always have rooms available." I said OK and thanked him and told him to have a good night and walked to the motel next door. When I got inside I said the same thing: "One bed for two nights, please." The lady was behind a glass screen and slid the window open. "Identification please." I reached into my purse and gave her my ID, she started typing on the computer in front of her then frowned and made a smacking noise with her teeth. "We don't have any availability tonight," then she slid me my ID back and said, "Sorry." I told her no problem and told her to have a good night. I walked back to my car and went to another hotel that was nearby but when I got out of my car and went to the door there was a sign up saying "Gone for break."

    I should've just gone back home to the basement

but I really just wanted to be alone and to detoxify myself from smoking and doing dumb things I had no business doing. I walked back to my car and drove to an abandoned building parking lot, turned off my lights then parked. I kept my car running so I could feel the heat, I remembered that I had my pillow and blanket in my bag so I quickly jumped to the back seat and pulled them out. I laid my pillow on my back seat and spread out my blanket on top of me. Trying to make myself cozy I stretched my legs out to the front seat then closed my eyes trying to fall asleep. A highway was right by the parking lot and all I could hear was cars howling in the wind as they sped by. The noise was peaceful but it kept me from falling asleep, so I got up to grab my phone in the passenger seat. Even though the screen was half green and cracked all over, I could still surprisingly see on the phone and type. The glass got in my fingers but if I touched it lightly it didn't hurt as bad. I looked up "calming rain sounds" and played it to tune out the highway noise. I finally was dozing off. In my mind I kept thinking to myself about what happened with Ronald. This thought kept me up. I went to the front seat to turn my car off then I lay back down and I kept replaying how he did me and it made me angry at myself. I didn't know what to do to stop this way of thinking so I started to pray. I prayed for God to comfort me in this situation and help me be wiser when it comes to making decisions and listen to my gut when it's telling me something isn't right. I breathed out through my right nostril for five seconds then let it out through my left then breathed out through my left for seven seconds, then let it out through my right. I took a final deep breath through my mouth to my stomach and held it for seven seconds and let it out. I started to feel a weight lifted off my back and my mind became clear.

    I woke up the next morning early around Eight o'clock and thankful. My phone was still playing rain sounds so I turned it off. I got out of the car, stretched my arms and legs to the sky, then opened up the driver's door and pushed my seats up and started my car. I heard of a phone repair place that wasn't too far so I headed there. It was December 2019, there wasn't any snow out but it still was cold outside. Around 28 degrees from what my car thermometer was telling me. I had my heat on and windows down while one hand was out the window. I didn't even care to smoke any more. And I damn sure didn't want to go back to that basement, I didn't even have a window down there except for the basement windows where you only see the ground through these tiny clear cubes. So things like simply feeling the wind while driving felt so good to me. When I got to the phone repair store parking lot, I rolled my windows up and before leaving the car took a deep breath in through my right nostril observing in as much oxygen as I could to my right side of my body and holding my left nostril, then did the same with my left nostril while holding my right nostril then took a deep breath through my mouth letting that cold air get to my stomach. It felt refreshing. I was refreshed and was ready to start my day. I still was upset about what happened yesterday and had my regrets but I wasn't going to let these emotions take over my day today.

    I got out of my car and closed my door then walked inside the phone repair store.

A skinny guy with long dark brown hair and glasses was in the back working on someone's phone. He was taking the screen apart and without looking up said, "I'll be right with you in a few minutes," while he continued to work. "No problem," I said while checking the store out. There were phone cases on the walls and a glass clear table with phones inside that were damaged and some even had been fixed. "Alrighty, what brings you in?" he said. I told him about what happened with my phone, then he gave me a quote on how much it would be and how long it would take for him to repair my phone. It was going to be an hour for him to fix it. I told him I'll be back by then and thanked him, then left the store. The mall wasn't too far so I decided to walk over there and do some window shopping. I looked around at the bridal stores looking at dresses. I love these stores. I think it's just the dress selections that make me feel like a princess. After looking around there I went to the food court and ended up stuffing my face with these chicken fingers, fries and restaurant ranch. I love it when restaurants make homemade ranch. It's always the best. I also had a side of a large blue pop to wash my food down, it was so cold and delicious when I got done drinking it. After I got done eating I put my food tray on top of the garbage can where the other ones were and went back to get my phone. When I got inside of the phone store I playfully shouted, "I'm back," and laughed. "Hey, your phone is done, he said and handed me my phone and it had a clear wrapping around it. I paid and thanked him and went back to my car with my phone in my hand this time holding it carefully.

Chapter 5 : giving additional efforts

Nearby was a hotel so I decided to stop by to see if they had any rooms available. I parked in the parking lot in front of the hotel then went inside to the counter for "one room for one night." At this point if they didn't have any rooms available I was just gonna go back home to the basement and suck it up. She said "Yes" and asked for my ID and said they had a $50 deposit. I got my room key and was so grateful. I grabbed my bag out of the car and walked back into the lobby to head to my room. This hotel wasn't the best in town but to me it was. I walked up the side stairs to get to my room. My room was on the second floor. When I got inside my room I went to the bathroom to wash my hands then brushed my teeth. After getting settled in and putting my bag down and taking a shower I got hungry again and went to get a sub from the gas station that was walking *distance. I got a sub with some chips and a water bottle. I walked back to my room and ate my sub while looking out the window. In my view I could see trees and a big freeway. I ate my sub with the window open enjoying the cold air. A cat by the window came walking by, since I was on the second floor I dropped down some chips for him to eat. At first the cat ran when he looked up and saw chips falling down. But the next day I looked out the window and all the chips were gone.*

The next day after checking to see if the cat ate the chips I just decided to go back home. My twenty-first birthday was coming up and I had planned to do a photo shoot and had to get my birthday cake and balloons. I gathered my things and headed to the lobby to give the guy at reception my room key then headed to my car with my bag. On the way home I stopped by a bakery shop and got my cake. When I got inside the bakery they didn't have much to choose from. So I just made do with what they had. I saw a plain white cake and asked, "Could you put a rainbow on this cake and put '21 Bambii '?" The baker said she could but it would be an extra charge and I told her, "Thats fine, I still want it, thank you." While she added that I thought to myself what else did I want to put on my cake and thought, Strawberry around the top and colorful sprinkles around the side.

When she was done I loved my cake so much I wanted to never eat it. It was for my family to eat but I had to bring it to the photo shoot so I could have that picture of it with me. Sometimes you have to create your own colorful rainbow when your life is full of storms. After she got done with my cake, I paid for it then left.

I went to the market and got my strawberries. After leaving the market I headed back home and before I walked in I breathed to twenty-two, I held my right nostril then breathed deep in for five seconds then let it go through my left nostril while holding my right and then repeated that until I got to twenty-two. I gave myself a talk before going in: Look this is temporary, don't give up on looking for a place of your own. Maybe the reason these places weren't allowing you to move there is because God has something better for you. I had to keep faith in my heart. I also had to get my outfit ready, I had a purple glitter bra and a long purple skirt. Giving snazzy twenty-

one vibes. I put my outfit in my bag and my two-inch heels that I loved and went upstairs to wash off the strawberries that I bought and had put into the refrigerator when I came in that was right by my cake. After I got done washing them I added them around my cake. I had extra ones left so I just took them downstairs in the basement and ate them. The next day I did my photo shoot for my birthday and made a blog: "My 21st birthday vlog, the meaning of my tattoo and more." For my birthday I went out to eat with my family. A few days after my birthday was New Year's. I spent New Year's with my family, we played games, performed karaoke and did the countdown.

I enjoyed myself until my aunt called me the wrong pronoun and it made me go sit alone at the dining room table. When my feelings are hurt it's hard for me to not show it through my face or eyes because they start to water and my hormone pills only make me more emotional about these types of situations. I know that not everyone is gonna be accepting of me and I had to realize that but when I'm around family I just want to be around love and hear my pronouns I identify with, not with the ones they see me as. The next day on January 1st, 2020, I got into a horrible fight with a loved one. This family member, we always have or ups and downs from good cheerful times as a kid to very dark times that made me question if this family member had good intentions toward me. Throughout everything I love this family member and I never will stop. The fight started because I told this family member about how my aunt misgendered me, and how I don't like to be around people who don't truly support and love me for me. When I was telling this family member about how this made me feel, the family member felt as if I was being dramatic for getting upset. I always felt like this family member had a thing against me identifying as a trans woman too so I just blankly asked, "Do you have a problem with me being transgender?" She got mad and flipped it around and one thing led to another. She was saying very disrespectful things to me and told me I was dead to her and that she had a mental funeral for me. My mom had to hold her back from coming into my face and my younger sister was holding me back. She kept getting closer and closer to me while my mom was holding her back by the door. She kept threatening me saying she was gonna stab me, which is something she already did to me when I was in eighth grade. I still have the scar on my leg. She finally got loose from my mom and clawed at my face. It felt as if a cat had clawed at my face from her nails ripping into my skin. After she did that we started fighting. After we stopped fighting she left out in her car and I went to open the garage to leave out in my car. I didn't want to be fighting with this family member, I hate when we don't talk. I looked at her sad because I love this family member so much. I just wish we had a different bond because it's like when we are cool and everything is going well it goes well. But when things are bad between us they turn bad. We didn't talk for nine months after that. One day my younger sister was on the phone with her and I just said hey to this family member and we started talking again. I never hold grudges toward anyone. I wanted us to talk sooner but I felt it was best we didn't. I knew from a young age to always forgive and never have hate in your heart toward anyone. My great-grandmother always would hold my hands telling me to stay sweet and those words meant everything to me.

    Months went by and I was still in the basement. I had been applying to places still constantly and wasn't getting any callbacks. I kept applying to different houses, townhomes and apartments because I needed to get out of this basement. It started to get overwhelming; one day while I was sleeping I heard water dripping and I woke up instantly and turned my head to see that it was coming from the water tank. There was a big puddle of water by the tank and I thought it would stay over there and wouldn't spread so I just went back to sleep. I woke up two hours later and the entire basement was flooded. My clothes that I had piled up in bags were soaked and my rugs that I sat down on the floor were soaked and most of my belongings. I stepped out of my bed that was on the floor and it felt like I was outside. I quickly went upstairs and told my mom about the basement. We went down back to the basement to move around some of her stuff that was down there and move around my rugs so the water could go down the drains that were blocked. Then I put my bed up against the wall. For a few days while letting the water go down the drain I slept on the living room couch. It took three days for all that water to go down the drain. By that time my rugs were ruined and most of my clothes had gone moldy. It smelled like a swap down there. After that I decided to get storage totes and put all my clothes in them. Just in case the basement wanted to flood again my stuff wouldn't get damaged. While shopping at the store to get my storage totes I went by the home appliances and got myself home decorative pictures to put on my walls for when I move, also silverware and plates. I still wasn't getting any calls back from the places I applied for but I just felt like I wouldn't be there for long and to have hope.

When I would get down about staying in the basement and people would come over and I would hear them stomping over my head, I would just look in my storage totes where I kept my home appliances and get happy. A couple more months went by and I was still in my same situation trying to stay positive in a place I really didn't want to be, so I decided to leave my phone on my bed and go for a bike ride to clear my mind. I was on my bike for the whole day riding up hills that were bumpy then getting to the top of the hill then cruising down them closing my eyes and breathing in all that fresh air. After being outside all day on my bike it was starting to get dark out and I dreaded going back home. I just really disliked being in that basement. I felt shut off from everyone in the house because they all had rooms with windows and didn't have to hear the floors make noise over their head. All I had was my candles and patience to keep telling myself that this is temporary, but I felt that was running low. Thinking about that made me ride my bike slowly going home. When I finally got home I put my bike in the garage and went downstairs to the basement and grabbed my phone off my bed. When I checked my phone notifications I had a missed call and a voicemail. When I listened to the voicemail I got news that I got approved from an apartment complex and they were calling me back to let me know that I could come there tomorrow and give them a deposit so I could move in.

Chapter 6 : inner thoughts..

What I noticed on this journey is how important inner dialogue is. If you can dream something you want in your head, you can make that happen, all you need to do is have patience and believe. Whenever I'm feeling down I let myself know that it's OK to take a break just as long as you don't give up on yourself. I take a couple of steps back, regain my composure and ask myself OK what is the next step? Then try my best to strive for that. Failure is OK, at least you can say you tried rather than doubting yourself and never doing anything to change your situation. Forgiveness, patience, gentleness, kindness, grace and discipline is what I try to live by. I made some pretty bad decisions in my life that I used to let determine my future, but not anymore. I am a flawed human being. As long as you learn from your past, you can make your future awesome.

God is a way maker and we all have his blood running through our body. Feel your emotions, every single one, they might be telling you something important, but don't let them take over you. Breathe in and out until you get it right. Slay until your hair turn grey... and have patience until your hair turn grey also if you not slaying then what the F***k are you saying?

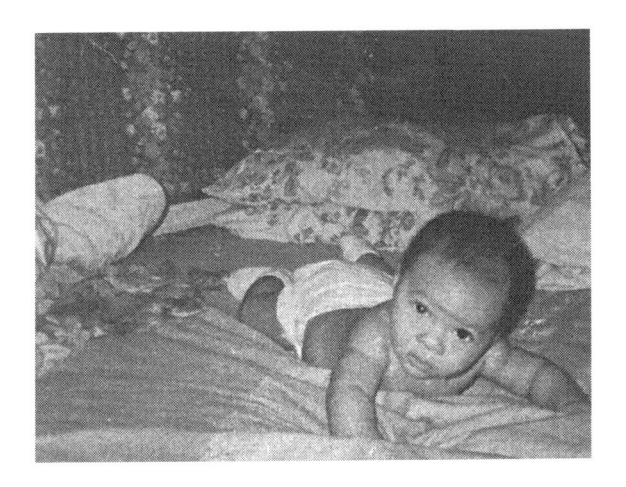

Baby I t s b a m b i i

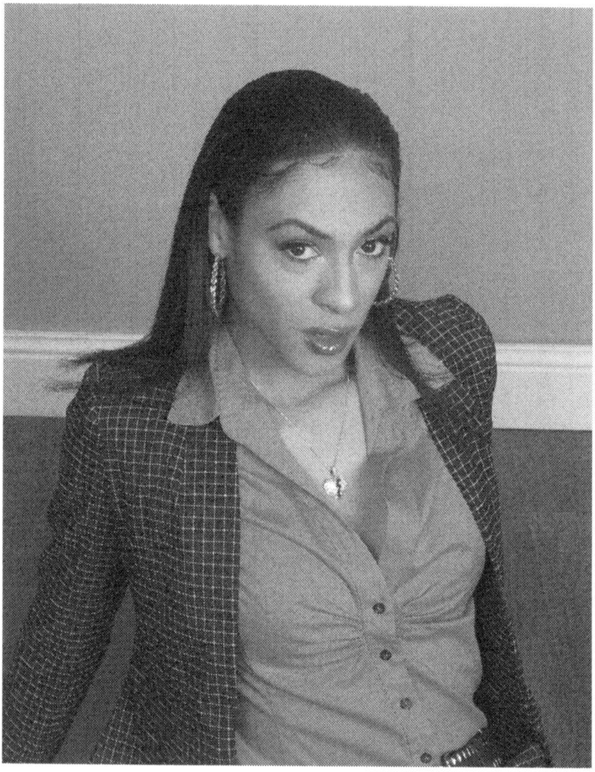

2011   2020

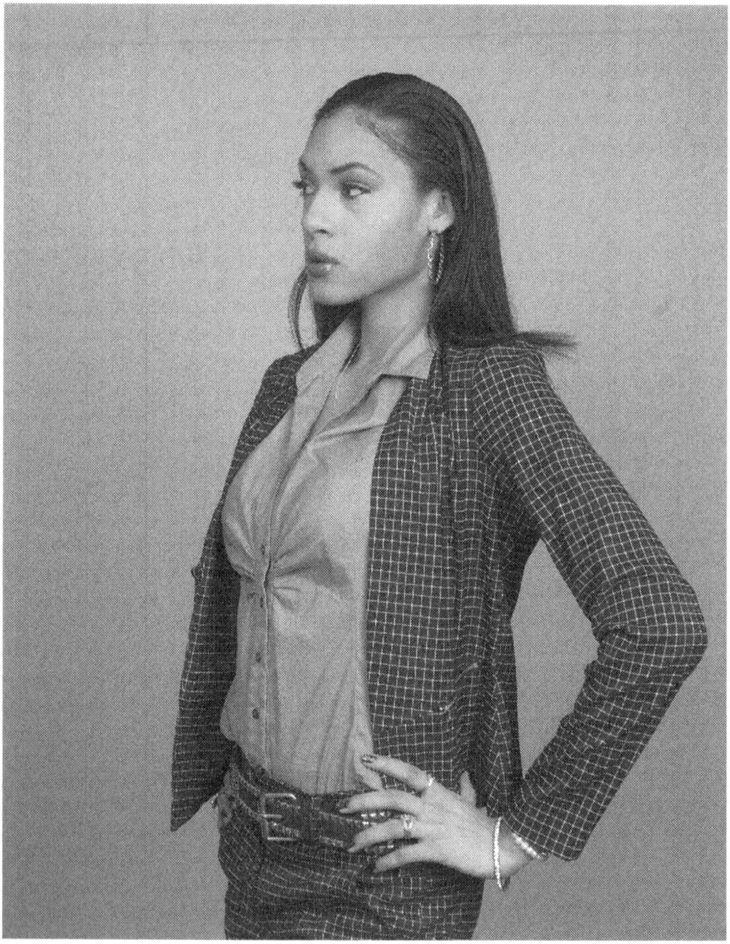

2012   2020

Selena also known as bam
I dedicate this book to anyone that is
going through a rough time..trust me I know

you feel...keep your head to the sky & when you want to give up go a little harder, transform your discouraging thoughts to a delicate flower.

- I t s b a m b i i playhouse

Patience until your hair turn grey ...

Slay until your hair turn grey..

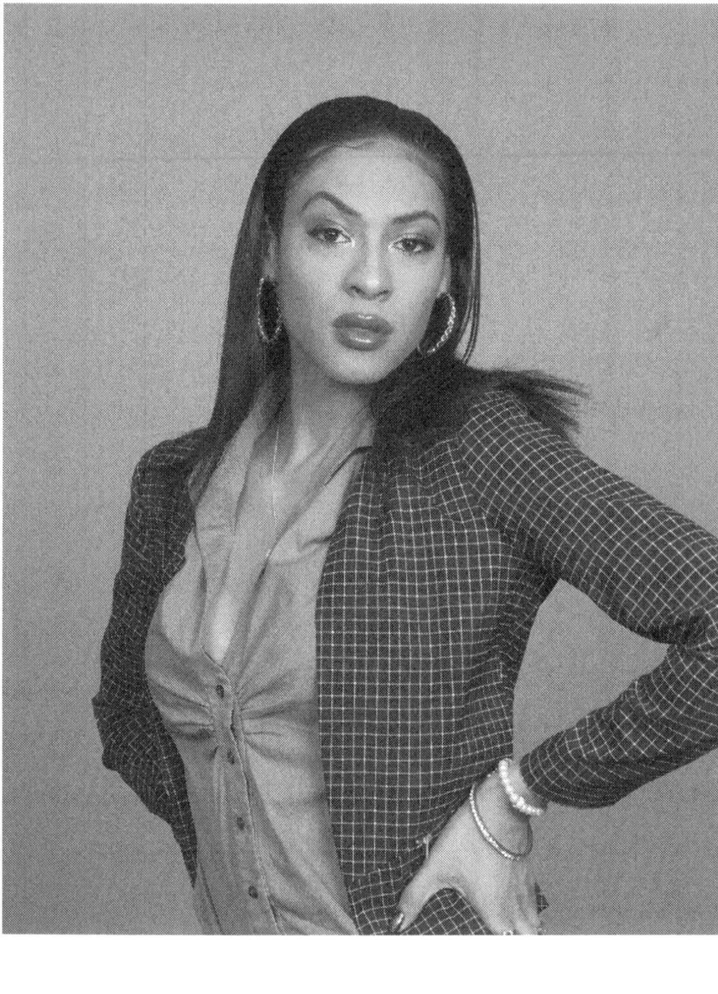

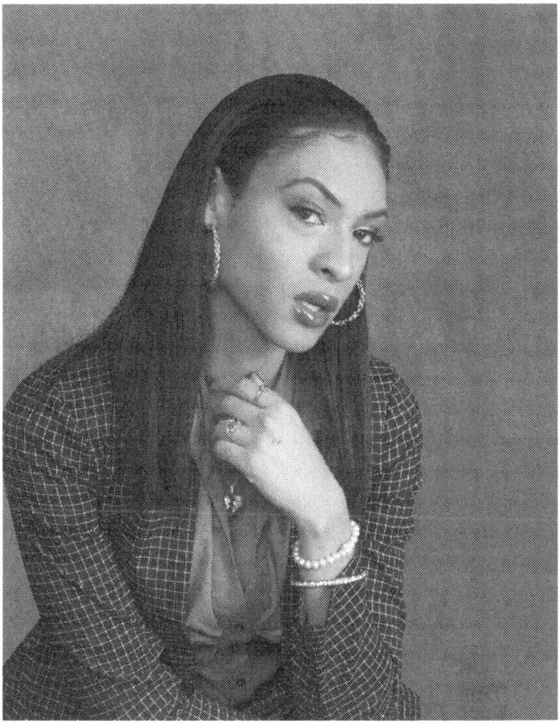

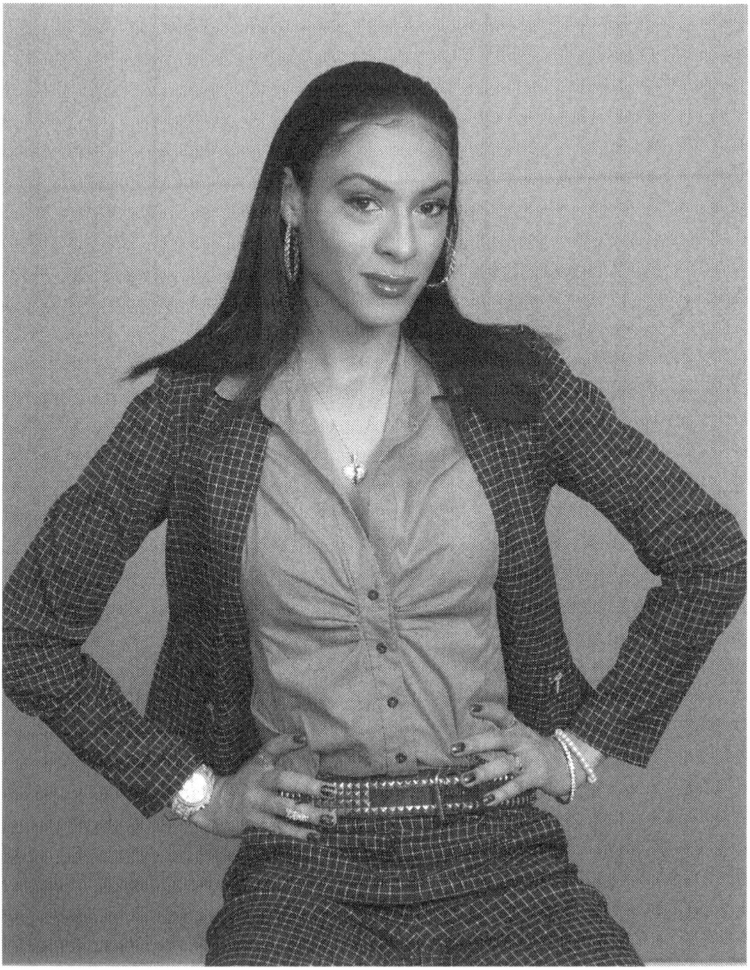

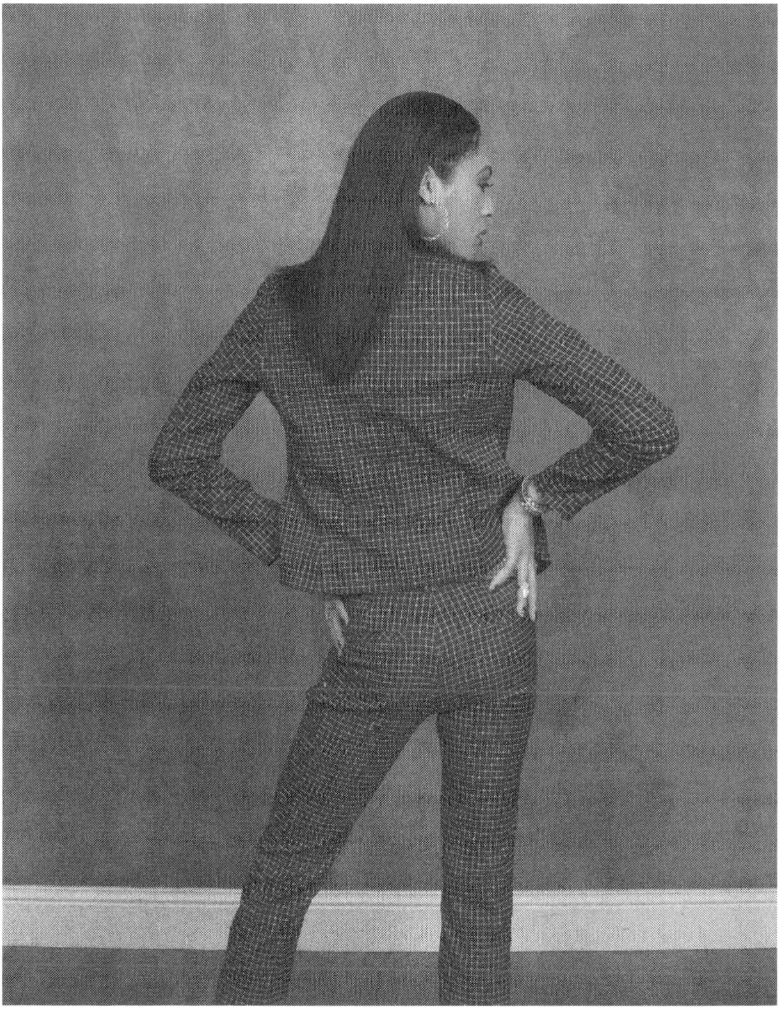

Manufactured by Amazon.ca
Bolton, ON